AF348437

Isaac Mason

Life of Isaac Mason as a Slave

e-artnow 2020

Isaac Mason

Life of Isaac Mason as a Slave

Autobiography of a Fugitive Slave

e-artnow, 2020
Contact: info@e-artnow.org

ISBN 978-80-273-0869-9

Contents

Worcester, Mass., July 19, 1893.

I have known Isaac Mason very well since 1850. He has done a great deal of work for me and my household. I know him to be an honest, faithful and intelligent man. I have not had time to examine his book in manuscript, but I am sure his statements may be trusted, and that his experience will prove very interesting. I hope his book will have a good sale, and commend it to the public.

Geo. F. Hoar.

PREFACE.

Having repeatedly been asked by my many friends to write the history of my life as a slave, especially by some who have heard me lecture on certain portions of that ever memorable period of my life, I have, after some hesitation as to its advisability, reluctantly concluded to accede to their wishes, and now present to them a truthful sketch of my eventful life in the dark days of slavery. As these checkered scenes of my early life reflectively present themselves to my mind at my advanced state of life, I wonder how I withstood all the abuse and cruelty of these early years. Our lives are largely composed of sorrow and joy, but my cup, it seems to me, has been full to overflowing with sorrow, but God has been my strength and my salvation, and has brought me thus far in the journey of life, and in him I trust, praying that, in his good time he will take me to that heavenly home where our earthly trials will cease and where there will be no more sorrow.

My story is told in a plain matter-of-fact way, and I hope my readers will overlook and excuse the defects which must necessarily abound throughout the book, owing to lack of educational advantages.

ISAAC MASON.

CHAPTER I
EARLIEST RECOLLECTIONS.

In Kent County, in the northern part of the State of Maryland, there was at the time of my earliest recollections (and I suppose it yet remains), a small town known as George Town Cross Oats, having a population of about 500 or 600. It was in this town, on the 14th day of May, 1822, AD, that I inhaled my first supply of air, that my eyes, for the first time, were brought in contact with the beautiful light surrounding the terrestrial world, the earthly home of mankind, and the first sound of my infant voice was raised in shrill cries for a mother's tender care and parental affection. This was the place of my nativity and the date of my birth. It was also the time that my mistress became the owner of one more slave and so much richer by my birth. My mother was, unfortunately, numbered in the family of slavedom, belonging to one Mrs. Hannah Woodland, and according to the institution of slave law, I legally, or illegally, became her property. Though my father was a free man still he had no claim to me. My mother's name was Sophia Thompson, and she served in the capacity of house servant. She was the mother of five children, four sons and one daughter, of whom I was the first born, and William Anderson, of the city of Worcester, Mass., the second. My father, Zekiel Thompson, was, as I said, a free man, and most of his time served as a farm hand on one of the farms owned by my mistress. Whether from his activity and knowledge of farm work or as an inducement to remain near his wife, I do not know, but he was permitted to hold the position of overseer of the work and farm hands.

My mistress, Mrs. H. Woodland, was a widow-her husband being a sea captain and lost at sea before I was born or had any knowledge of him. They were both natives of Scotland. He owned two farms, and at his death his wife became the owner of both, carrying on business until the time of her death. She was the mother of five children, one son and four daughters. The son, Samuel Woodland, who was said to be rich, owning two farms, several houses, and from one hundred to one hundred and fifty slaves, was, as near as language can express it, a lifetime tyrant to his farm hands and house servants. His tyranical passion was so great that on the day of his death he called in the men from their work, and with a stick in his dying hand struck each one across their hands. As each one received the parting gift he had to file out and another take his place. This ceremony continued to within two hours of his death, when from exhaustion he had to cease. Those who were on the end of the line of march on that day fortunately lost their master's parting blessing. My mistress was naturally of a good disposition, just the reverse of her son, or he from her. My grandfather (my mother's father) had charge of the farm hands and all that pertained to the farm, as he was considered faithful and trustworthy. The principal products of the farms were corn, wheat and oats. Infant years rapidly passed by and the time drew near when little Will, *alias* Isaac, had to leave his mother's knee and childish play to enter upon the duties of serving his owners.

Accordingly, when between five and six years of age, I was assigned to the duties of housework, to wait on my mistress and to run errands. When she went out driving I had to accompany her in the capacity of a page, to open the gates and to take down guard fences for her to drive through. That I might be found at night as well as by day my sleeping apartment was in her chamber on a truckbed, which was during the day time snugly concealed under her bedstead and drawn out at night for the reposing place of Isaac's weary body while he dreamed of days yet to come. I remained in this distinguished position until I was about fifteen years old, when a change in common with all slave life had to be made either for the better or for the worse.

On the day that proved to be her last to be spent on this earth I was required to accompany her on a visit to the farm, the second farm, which was not so frequently visited, where she spent the afternoon in looking over the stock and products which detained her until towards evening. Her examinations were completed and she returned home. This visit was made in the gig drawn by the old black mare. My place was, as customary, by her side. We arrived home about seven o'clock in the evening. She told me to "take care of the old mare"; that meant to unharness and put her in the stable, and when I had completed my task to "come to her, as she wanted me to go on an errand." I obeyed her orders and went direct to her chamber, where I found her lying on the floor in an unconscious state and unable to speak.

I immediately ran down stairs and informed my mother how I had found mistress. She sent me at once after Mrs. Island, a daughter of Mrs. H. Woodland, who lived about half a mile from us. Upon hearing the sad news she hurried with me back to the house and sent for the doctor. He lost no time in attending to the call, and did all he could to restore her to consciousness and life, but his medical skill failed to produce a favorable result. About 11 o'clock that night she died, as the doctor said, from a stroke of paralysis. The last words she was known to utter were the orders she gave me that evening. Thus ended the life of mistress at the age of ninety years.

My grandfather, Richard Graham Grimes, was sent down that night to a place called Morgan's Creek, to a man by the name of Hugh Wallace, to come up immediately and make arrangements for the funeral. His first wife was the daughter of my mistress. He lost no time in answering the summons and attended to all the necessary requirements for the obsequies, and on the third day after her death my mistress was consigned to mother earth.

At last the day dawned when this group of slaves had to part, not only from the old homestead but from each other, and to go to scenes and climes unknown to them. At last the sunshine was passing and the gloom fast overspreading. Mother and children, brothers and sisters to separate, perhaps forever.

The farm with all of its contents were left, for the time being, under the care and supervision of my grandfather. He continued to hold charge till July of the same year, about the space of three months, at which time Mr. H. Wallace appeared on the estate to make arrangements for settling the affairs. Everything belonging to the estate excepting the slaves were sold. The farm with its contents was bought by a man by the name of Isaac Taylor. My grandfather, in consideration of his old age and the time being past for useful labor, was *handsomely* rewarded with his freedom, an old horse called the "old bay horse" —which was also past the stage of usefulness-and an old cart; but, alas! no home to live in or a place to shelter his head from the storm.

My father, as I said before, was a free man and had the privilege of purchasing my mother and my sister, who was then about a year old, for $600. My mother at this time was in very ill health, and it was thought by many she could not live very long. My father not being able to pay the amount asked, had to find a sufficient security before he could obtain a bill of sale. He was fortunate enough to find that assistance in the person of Dr. Hyde, with whom I was soon to become personally acquainted. The remainder of the slaves each received a note from the hands of Mr. H. Wallace, and were directed by him to carry it to a certain person named by him, which act showed that each slave had been previously disposed of. Some were sold and some were hired out for a certain time to pay debts due by the estate.

I received my little note and was told to carry it to Dr. Hyde, who was living in the same place where I was born. I was not sold, but only hired out to pay a small bill of $25 which would not take very long as regards to time, but by an economical table of work I was destined to fill the place of more than one servant. The Doctor and his considerate wife were determined to utilize my whole time in their service. My work at this place consisted in cooking, washing, sweeping, taking care of the horses, attending to the garden, which contained about half an acre of land, and milking two cows. The good training of my former mistress had very materially fitted me for the varied duties of this house. By hard work early and late I could accomplish my daily tasks.

Some persons may suppose that by accomplishing all this work in one day would satisfy an employer, master or mistress, but satisfaction was hard to find. I was only the property of another, working to pay the debt of another, who I suppose thought he ought to receive interest on his bill; and that interest had to be paid by me in addition to the daily labor, by receiving a whipping every day besides losing a meal-either a breakfast, a dinner, or a supper-according to their best judgment. Some may wonder which I regretted most, the whipping or the meal.

I sorrowed the loss of the meal more than anything else. To me this certainly was a great punishment.

The last day I stayed with the Doctor he told me that he wanted me to stay at home for he was going away and would not be back till after nightfall. I had made arrangements with some other boys to go rabbit hunting. Knowing it was Christmas week, and I was not bound to stay there, as my time was out, I concluded to have my rabbit hunt as agreed; so off I went with my associates. I did not get back to the house till after dark. Wanting to complete my day's work before the Doctor arrived I made my way into the kitchen, as I thought unseen by any person, to get the milk pail which was always kept in there, and milk the cows. Mrs. Hyde, the Doctor's wife, saw me, skipped out from somewhere and locked the kitchen door behind me. This was not a very pleasant situation, for a slave and the mistress to be locked up in the same room. She had a purpose in view, but I had none just then; my future actions had to be governed by what she was about to do. She told me to take off my coat so that she could give me a whipping for going off. According to her orders I obeyed; then she commenced work in right good earnest with her well roasted hickory wottels. Their smarting pains did not feel pleasant on my head and shoulders, so I laid hold of them and contested my strength with the fair feminine tyrant. In the struggle for victory I managed to jerk her down to the floor, and before she could regain her feet I jumped out of the window; and as the Doctor had not yet arrived home I made good my safety.

I went to the barn and crept away under the back part of the hay, where I knew I would be secure for the night. I stayed there lamenting over my stripes till midnight; then I came out and went to my mother's, which was about half a mile off. She told me the Doctor had been there hunting for me. Thinking he might soon return I did not stay there very long. I next started off for my grandfather's, which was about four miles away. I found him at home and he let me in. I did not learn that my pursuer had been to this place, so I thought myself safe for a while. He told me he had received a letter from Mr. H. Wallace directing him to bring me down to Morgan's Creek, as the Doctor had nothing more to do with me and that I was going to another place.

Next morning grandfather arose, shelled a bushel of corn and was going to Headchester to dispose of it for other necessary comforts, telling me I might go along with him. Soon the old bay horse and cart, the legacy from the Woodland estate, were hitched together and started on the journey. On our way I was surprisingly met by the Doctor on horseback. As soon as I saw him I crouched down in the bottom of the old cart thinking to avoid him, but I was much mistaken. His keen eye had caught sight of me, and no doubt his breast was burning with revenge on account of his wife having to kiss the kitchen floor. He drew near to my hiding-place and strove his best to cut me with his horsewhip, but he missed me. I jumped out of the cart and hid in the fields till I thought he was gone. When I came out of my hiding-place he could not be seen, so I joined the old man in the cart once more, pursuing our journey. He told my grandfather, "If he did not have me back to his house before four o'clock that day he would have an officer after me and have me back." The officer failed to come, consequently I have not seen the Doctor nor his wife since.

This Doctor Hyde had become security for the payment of the $600 required from my father for the purchase of my mother and sister. He was so much enraged on account of this trouble with me, that he demanded immediate payment of the money. This brought a gloom over my father and mother's humble but happy home. He had no money nor the means of getting it. The spiteful bondsman could soon find the way to get it, and that was by selling mother and sister. This means was well understood by them, and plans were considered to avoid this sacrifice when mother resolved to take her young child and flee to Baltimore, Md. Her conclusions were soon put in practice, and it was not long before she found herself and child in that famous city. There she found a philanthropic Quaker, who had saved a great number of families from being separated under such circumstances. He told her he would furnish her with the money if her husband would make out a bill of sale for the child she had with her. She sent father word of what she found in way of a partial relief. The opportunity was readily embraced by him and he hastened to Baltimore and gave the bill of sale for my sister, which was to last till she was eighteen years old. My parents further agreed that in the event of my sister's death before the expiration of that time, they were to finish out the time or give sufficient work to the value of the amount. All was finally settled and they returned to George Town Cross Oats, minus their only daughter that they had to sell to save themselves. My father had paid H. Wallace $200 down, which left $400 to be raised by the Quaker. To the great astonishment of the Doctor father called and paid the amount. He was so much perplexed that he wanted to know where the money came from-supposing it had been stolen. My sister remained with the Quaker family till she was sixteen years old, when they gave her two years off her time. This generous friend sent for my father to come to Baltimore and emancipate both my mother and sister, as they were sold under debt. He did so, and consequently they were all three free people according to the laws of the State of Maryland.

To return to my own personal narrative-by jumping from the old cart to escape from Dr. Hyde and rejoining grandfather. We rode on to Headchester, which is now known as Millerton, remained there until night and then returned home. I stayed there all night and next morning after breakfast we started for Morgan's Creek, which was to be my new home. We had to ride a distance of twenty-two miles, arriving there about night. This was New Year's eve. I had an uncle living at this place by the name of Joe Grimes. His wife lived in Chestertown with the same man I was destined to live with. Mr. H. Wallace gave Uncle Joe a note, with instructions to deliver it and Isaac into the hands of Mr. James Mansfield, jr. He arrived there about eight o'clock that night, a distance of three miles, when I for the first time saw my new master. His wife was named Mary. They had two children —a girl and a boy; the former was about five years of age and the latter three years. He was a cabinet-maker by trade and worked with his father who followed the same business. He very soon bought his father out, taking the business into his own hands, and began to thrive very rapidly.

CHAPTER II
IN A NEW HOME.

Chestertown was quite a thriving place, having five thousand or more inhabitants, and was the county seat for Kent County. It bordered on the Chesapeake Bay, where we had ready transportation to Baltimore, Md., three or four times a week. There were a large number of wealthy families living there at that time who owned large plantations. On being introduced to my master the next morning I was informed what I was expected to do. I was told that I was coming sixteen years old the next spring, and he had bought me for the special purpose to work about the house and to do whatever was wanted of me; and, also, I was expected to do what I was set about, and to do it well and quick. He said he would not overlook one fault. If I did as he said I would be properly treated; if I did not I would get the hickory wottel. I assured him faithfully I would do the best I could. I found that my work was precisely the same as that I had performed at Dr. Hyde's, my last place, so I got along for the first two weeks very nicely. I gave them satisfaction, as I thought; they, that is my master and his wife, appeared pleased. I concluded I was all right and was going to have a nice time at my new home. At this time there was not the dread of a daily whipping and the loss of one meal a day. It was not long before I was to learn that storms followed calms, and war came after peace.

One Friday morning, after being there about four weeks, I well remember the day, I was busy at work on my hand-irons. My mistress came out and wanted to know what I had been doing all the morning. I turned round and looked at her, and saw that her face was awfully red; there was something wrong but I could not divine it. She hurriedly went out of the room where I was, into the back room, and got her cowhide; without the least ceremony she lit on me-the same as a hungry hawk on an innocent chicken. Her descent upon me was so sudden that I did not know what to do. I begged, I entreated her to stop; but she grew worse and worse. The blows came faster and faster, and every one brought the blood streaming from my head and back till I was covered from head to foot. Being a large, fleshy woman, she at last became fatigued and exhausted, and had to quit her inhuman chastisement. I was so unmercifully beaten that I was unfit for work that day.

Next morning I could not stand up I was so weak and exhausted from loss of blood. My eyes and head were completely swollen, and for a few days I had to remain a poor sufferer-the victim of a woman's spite and hatred for a poor despised race. What I had done to deserve all this treatment I knew not. Here I was, no one to care for me, no one to console me. After awhile I got so that I could resume work. She never repeated that kind of treatment again, but consigned me to a worse fate for the future —I may say for a limited period. Whenever I did anything that was considered wrong after that I had to go to the cellar, where I was stripped naked, my hands tied to a beam over head, and my feet to a post, and then I was whipped by master till the blood ran down to my heels. This he continued to do every week, for my mistress would always find something to complain of, and he had to be the servant of her will and passion for human blood. At last he became disgusted with himself and ceased the cruel treatment. I heard him tell her one day-after he had got through inflicting the corporal punishment-that he would not do it any more to gratify her.

One day, to my great astonishment, I found that my work was to be changed from a domestic servant to a farm hand. Having been trained to do a little of both it did not seem hard for me to work at either. Mr. Mansfield had purchased a little farm a few years before I went to live with him, containing sixty acres. It cost him three dollars an acre, and was very poor land. I, together with an older hand, was placed on this farm to work. It was about a mile out of Chestertown and had no house or barn on it, so we had to travel the distance four times a day to get meals and to feed the horses. Having to carry manure to the farm we had the privilege of riding there and back every time. I continued to work on this farm a little over five years. When we commenced reaping the first year it yielded only from five to six bushels of corn and wheat to the acre; after five years it yielded thirty bushels to the acre. The last three years I worked on the farm it was under my charge.

Besides attending to the work of the farm I had to drive the hearse which conveyed the dead to the grave, for my master being a cabinet-maker, was also an undertaker. I had to attend the funerals of all the prominent men and women within a radius of twenty miles of that place. My boss had so much confidence in me that he would send me twenty miles alone with a coffin to bury some great person, and I would be gone, sometimes, as long as two days. He was the only man in that town that attended to such business. On one occasion I went to bury the wife of a high sheriff, and to my surprise and confusion found that all the men were drunk. When they arrived at the burying ground they were just fit for business-not to bury, but to quarrel. As they were removing the corpse from the hearse they let it fall to the ground, bursting open the coffin. They were in great confusion over it and I did not know how it would end. I drove off and left them, as my duties were ended. It was always customary on these funeral occasions, that after the burial a dinner was served to all who took part in the exercises —"rejoicing at the death." By this accident I lost my funeral dinner, as I fled for home not knowing what they might do to me if I remained-though the accident was no fault of mine; I was a slave, subject to anybody's insult and bad treatment.

During the five years and over that I worked on the farm I was never struck a blow. There was no one to find fault with my work. The boss was but seldom there and I was taken from under the control of my mistress. In the year 1845 I had done so well for my master, or at least he thought so-and I knew I had-that just before Christmas he told me to take the other man that was with me and shell out one hundred bushels of corn, and the same of wheat, and put them on board the sloop General Washington, to be taken to Baltimore. On the following Tuesday, after this was done, he gave me a new suit of clothes, and at ten o'clock we went on board the sloop and sailed for Baltimore to dispose of the corn and wheat. We arrived there the next morning, which was Wednesday. Mr. Mansfield went ashore and proceeded up town to see some friend of his, and left me at the vessel. Not receiving any orders from him I thought I would like to see something of the city; so off I started alone. While passing up Pratt Street I fell in with two men standing on the sidewalk. They were not standing close together. I could not very well pass around them, and to proceed I had to go between them, which I attempted to do. They soon stopped and severely beat me for so doing. When they got through my clothes were all full of blood that flowed from my own body. I was ignorant, yes, completely ignorant of their law, forbidding a negro from passing between two or more white men or women who were walking or standing on the sidewalk, and that he or she must take the street to give place to their superiors. By the time they got through inflicting their punishment I had learned something of the penalty of the crime. With my painful bruises and blood-stained garments I found my way back to the sloop to await the return of Mr. Mansfield. When he saw my unfortunate condition and had heard my pitiful story, he became quite indignant over it. He tried to obtain redress by offering a reward to discover the parties that had done the deed. To his astonishment, he was politely informed that his reward would do no good, as negroes are not allowed to pass between white men when they are standing talking. This is one of the methods they took to teach negroes their manners to white people. This was my first experience of a city walk.

Our freight was unloaded and disposed of, and on the following Friday we returned home. As usual, I resumed my customary work. Everything went along quite smoothly at the farm, at the hearse business, and at the house, until the month of August, 1846, when the golden dreams of my sunshine of peace began to draw near the horizon of that place I was doomed to call home; but I saw it not. Dark clouds were swiftly gathering over my head in uninterrupted succession for many days to come; but I discerned them not. The life of a slave is a wretched one in its best condition; if he always knew what awaited him in the future, it would be most wretched. He who holds the destiny of the world in His hands wisely hides from our eyes what a day may bring forth.

At this time the family became short of meat. We had two steers that had been turned loose in what was called the "common"—a tract of land about twelve miles off, containing two hundred acres of forest land—a pleasure and pasture ground for unused cattle. Another hand, with myself, was told to go to the common and capture one of the steers, and to bring it home to be slaughtered and packed away for the use of the family. According to orders we started on our journey, which was the last day of August. We labored hard all that day trying to find them, among a number of others, in the dense forest. As night began to set in we discovered our search, by the private mark that had been placed on them when they were put there. To our disappointment, the fast overspreading darkness prevented our capturing them that night, so we had to take the horses and return home, with the intention of renewing our labors early next day. At an early hour next morning we started on our journey. On our arrival we soon found our search, the lasso was thrown with steady, true aim, and the prize was captured. We mounted our horses and were soon on our way home-one leading and the other driving. Our captive did some considerable struggling for liberty, detaining us on the road so long that we did not reach home before four o'clock in the afternoon, when we were told to take him to Tom Carroll's slaughter house. At five o'clock he was slaughtered and hanging on the gallows, and by seven o'clock that night he was in the cellar, salted down and packed away for future use. In less than three days our supply of beef was completely spoiled, having maggots in it nearly as long as a little finger. A new life had come into it.

At this time my mistress had become the mother of another child; it was about two weeks old. She had stopping with her a young girl, a niece of hers, who performed the duty of housekeeper. She was the daughter of Hugh Wallace. When this miss of a housekeeper discovered the great calamity that had befallen the store of beef-making it unfit for the delicate stomachs of her aunt, uncle-in-law, cousins, and her own-she ordered that some of it be taken to the kitchen and boiled for the hands. After it had gone through the culinary department, its flavor and unpalatable taste made it too much for human stomachs of the strongest kind to endure. A slave's stomach was considered not to be human, but this undainty dish proved that it was. None of us could eat it. It had to be rejected because the stomach refused it. I was so bold as to cast my portion out to the dog, an act, I thought, unseen by any but those who were with me. I was mistaken; other eyes were on me but I knew it not then. This awful crime that I committed had at last sent my peace below the horizon, and the cloud had burst. The keen eye of the girlish housekeeper had seen it fall to the dog's mouth. Master, mistress and chief servant all agreed that I had been impudent to Miss Wallace, and of course I must pay the penalty. In Baltimore I was chastized for passing between two white men; now I am treated worse than that for casting rotten meat to a dog, because I could not force it down my throat when given me by my mistress' representative.

This remarkable event happened on a Saturday, at noon. Mr. Mansfield had that day gone away from home and was not to return before night. When he had been home but a short time he came out and met me in the yard, after I had put the horse up that he had been using, and wanted to know what I had done. Before I could think of any serious fault he picked up a stick four feet long and began to fire away at me with all his force, crying out, "What have you been doing?" I told him I had done nothing, and he exclaimed. "You are a liar!" He told me to go to the cellar and he would see. Though a slave, and his property, yet I dared to assert the lion of my manhood that he had aroused in me, and I replied, "I will not do it!" then he renewed the attack with the stick. I caught hold of it to prevent him from using it. He wrung and I twisted; he twisted and I wrung. At last I lost control of my temper and pushed him over a pile of wood that was in the yard. As he fell he cried out for Mary, his wife, to bring him his gun. Before she arrived with the deadly instrument I was over one fence and across the street. As I ascended the second fence to find refuge in the field he aimed his gun, firing three shots at me. The first shot grazed my head, removing a little hair; the second touched my ear, and the third passed through my hat; but they did not stop me from running. On reaching the mulberry thicket, where I thought I was safe, I stopped. I was ignorant of what I had so seriously done to cause all this. I remained here all that night.

At last Sunday morning dawned and found me hiding from the fierce anger of a man who would soon be making his way to church; but I could not go. I had no one to speak to but God. Alone, yet not alone. My thoughts may be somewhat surmised when I inform my readers of the sacred relationship of the man who had just attempted to take my life. He was a local preacher in the Methodist Church, and considered one of its most pious and consistent members. His religious fervor was so great that he could not content himself with his own church, but also identified his name with the colored Methodist Church of which I was a member. He would frequently attend our meetings, jump, shout and sing, like the rest of us. He was the leader of my class, my spiritual adviser and counsellor in the time of trouble. Now, by his merciless treatment, I am driven from the shelter of his home. What could I think of him? How could I judge of his religious profession? How could I receive his religious instructions? The more I thought of him this day the more my confidence in him grew weaker. He was my master, and by the inhuman law of slavery I was his property and must obey his mandates. During the day my hiding-place was discovered by a fellow-slave who brought me food, which removed a portion of sorrow from my wounded breast. In this affliction I found, as in former instances, that by turning my heart towards God, He would take care of me and provide for my wants. The Sabbath day drearily passed away, and night found me still among the mulberry bushes to spend a second night without shelter, bed or covering.

On Monday morning my *pious master* told one of the slave hands if he saw me to tell me to "come home!" When I received the message I immediately returned. On my arrival I met the would-be murderer, and he wanted to know "why I acted so; why I threw the meat to the dog?" In an instant the cause of Saturday's conflict and Sunday's sorrow came to my mind. Refusing to eat rotten beef and casting it to the dog had brought down his vengeance on my much-defenceless head. The secret was revealed. Miss Wallace had witnessed the act, taking it as a great insult to herself. To use his own expression: "It was an insult to Miss Wallace, for she had sent it out to the kitchen." I replied that I did not know it was an insult, I did not mean to insult her, and she did not know how bad it smelled. He abruptly told me to go to work and he would see about it. So we parted; he to counsel other methods of punishment or revenge, and I to my work on the farm. At this season we were busily engaged hauling lime to the farm. We completed this job in three weeks, then we had to gather in the corn and tread out some wheat. The treading was done by horses in what was called the "treading yard." It was about the middle of November when this portion of our annual work was completed.

The first important job that was assigned to Will (for my master always called me by that name), after finishing the farm work, was to take the horse and cart, with a note, and go to Mr. H. Wallace's for a barrel of turkeys and geese that were to be sent to Baltimore, Md. During all this time I had not heard anything about the spoiled meat trouble. I concluded it had all passed by, and to me almost forgotten. My conception of the trickery of mankind were very small at that time. If I had known the contents of the note, and what kind of poultry I was sent after, I would no doubt have been tempted to have resorted to my mulberry home, or some other more distant, but I did not. I had more lessons to learn. At two o'clock I started on my errand. The distance by the public road was ten miles, and it would be some time before I could return. I was acquainted with a road that would take me directly there, by crossing lands belonging to other persons, and the distance would not be more than three miles; so in order to economize time for the boss I took that route. This way I knew would bring me in contact with a creek a little below Mr. W's house. He always kept a boat on this creek, so that persons coming to or going from his house by that way could be ferried across by one of the slaves. The horse and cart were secured; I gave the signal and was soon safely landed on the other side. I inquired for the master of the mansion, and was directed to the treading yard. I soon found him, and delivered to him in person my trust and the message for the featherless and lifeless birds that were never to be seen. He gave me a pitchfork, telling me to shake up that straw, he would give me what I wanted pretty soon. I always endeavored to obey orders, so I complied by going to work with a good will pitching straw. I worked on, expecting every moment to receive the answer to my errand, but still it did not come. As it began to grow dark I became apprehensive that something was wrong. Finally, I told Mr. Wallace that I must be going home as I had work to do; would he please give me the turkeys and geese? He, to my great astonishment, struck me with his pitchfork with so much force that he broke it over my shoulders.

At this sudden change of affairs I suddenly started on the run, with he and his son after me like hounds in full chase after the fleeing fox. My safety depended upon my agile movements. My active feet did me good service and soon left my pursuers far behind. My impulsive thought was to flee directly home and secure the protection of him whom I was compelled to call master. Alas! alas! I was placing my trust in one who was betraying me, who was deceiving me; and soon I was to discover the blackness of his heart toward me. The vigorous efforts of the maddened foe pressed on me so great that the road for home had to be abandoned, and I had to flee to the dense woods for refuge. They were safely reached, and I could once more breathe easily. Here I remained till after midnight, when I thought I could venture out and try to find my way home. The great wonder was, how could I succeed. I knew Mr. W. always kept his boats in such a manner that I could get one and row across the creek; but then came the dread that they might be watching that means of escape and would capture me. That route had to be abandoned and another found. Blinded with grief and darkness I started up the creek in search of some shallow place where I might walk across. On I walked till at last I halted at a spot that I thought would do. The stream here was narrow; in I ventured. Step after step brought me into deeper water. Suddenly I found that I was beyond my depth. I could not swim, I could not go back. The scenes of death were before me. There was no one near by to call upon to save me. In the midst of my dilemma I remembered the Lord; upon Him with my whole heart I did call. If ever I prayed in my life I did this time. Soon my eyes became dim, my mind bewildered, and consciousness had departed from me. How long I remained in the water after that I know not. When consciousness returned I found myself safely resting on the opposite shore, wet and cold. My escape was miraculous, and I attributed it all to God.

Once more on terra firma I started for home, arriving there about four o'clock in the morning. I found that the horse and cart had arrived home during the night, having been brought there by one of Mr. Wallace's men. Next morning my boss met me when I was coming from the barn. He informed me that "Mr. W. was going to whip me for being impudent to his daughter in throwing that meat to the dog, and I had better have stayed and got it and had it over." I told him that I belonged to him, and if he wanted to do it I would submit—I did not want anybody else to do it. He bade me take off the wet clothes and put on the hearse clothes. I did so, and was quickly on my way with the hearse to the shop.

Though I was but a poor, despised slave, having no rights that I could call my own, even to the refusal of such food that I could not eat, yet I possessed that principle of true manhood to despise deceit in my employers. Here I found a man who had told me from time to time how to serve God, how to live right, and now had proved to be a base deceiver and a falsifier. Instead of the note asking for turkeys and geese, it was to whip me for what they deemed impudence. Could I believe him hereafter? Could I trust him any more? No! he had told me a lie. My confidence in him was gone, and my feelings towards him were changed. Was I happy or contented? No! for I did not know how soon another trap would be set for me to fall into the hands of my enemies. This uncertain state of mind was my daily, but yet unpleasant, companion. Its duration was uncertain. I would have felt somewhat at ease if the boss had inflicted this punishment, but he would not do it.

On December 15 Mr. Mansfield sent me down to the wharf to Jim Frisby, to get his scow, and proceed up to Mr. Wallace's and get ten cords of hickory wood. I was told to take another man with me. As I had to enter within the bounds of Wallace's estate again, I concluded to prepare myself for emergencies and a hasty retreat. I had come to know the trickery of the man I was dealing with and was determined to disappoint him. Jim Frisby was an old colored man who owned the scow, and he owned, besides, a small boat-just what was needed, and served my purpose admirably. While arranging for the scow I also bargained for the boat, taking care not to divulge my secret to any one. About ten o'clock we started on our journey. The distance was but five miles, the tide was running in our favor, and we were soon at our journey's end. We found the wood piled up on the shore ready for us. We began to load up the scow, but night came on us so fast that we could not finish. We took our lunch into the small boat and rowed to the other side of the creek, and sought out an old barn that I had frequently seen in that neighborhood, where we rested for the night. Being tired after our day's work we soon sought sweet sleep for our weary bodies.

Next morning we were both up by daylight and resumed our work, and by nine o'clock we were ready to return with our load of wood. My readers must not suppose that my eyes were idle while working here. My hands were working to serve Mansfield, and my eyes were working or watching to serve Will, *alias* Isaac. I knew my man, and I felt he was on the watch and only waiting for a chance to pounce down upon me. As we were preparing to start I looked up the road and saw Mr. W. coming towards the scow. I remarked to my fellow-workman that he was coming and there would be trouble for me. On he came with his silver-headed stick in hand. He drew near and jumped on board the scow, and I very deliberately stepped into Jim Frisby's little boat and struck out for the opposite shore. He was so sorely disappointed at his second defeat, that he took a keen aim at my head with his stick; but oh! he missed me and off I went. He tried another plan by sending two of his men in another boat after me, with instructions to bring me back dead or alive. I out-rowed them and jumped ashore with paddle in hand. I was making for a place of safety, but before I could secure myself they had overtaken me. Then a desperate struggle took place. They rushed for me. I dodged, threatening them to stand back or I would kill them. Still they tried to carry out the demand of the tyrant. In my struggles I looked on them as men in slavish bondage like myself, and executors of a master's will. They fought to obey him, I fought to save my body from bruises, and for aught I know, my life from sacrifice. Finding words of persuasion and threat of no avail, I brought my weapon down with full strength and true aim on the head of one of the attacking party, when he fell to the ground like a log. The other fellow ran off and left me to make good my flight from the avenger-not of blood, but of pretended impudence to his presumptuous daughter.

To return to the boat was impossible. To render assistance in carrying home the scow was out of the question. The way to Chestertown by land was the most convenient. As I drew near the house who did I see ride into the yard from a different direction but my mortal enemy, Mr. H. Wallace. He failed to see me, so I at once made a hasty retreat. To have gone nearer the house would have been as bad, if not worse, than staying on board the scow and having the unmerciful thrashing that was laid out for me. Moved by the impulse of the moment I turned around, made my way into the meadows and secured a position where I could see when he left the premises. These remarkable escapes from his hands were, to me, great miracles. I had formed a resolution that he should not beat me, and was determined to disappoint him at every attempt. He was aided by my cunning master, but I had no one to help me. Thus far success attended the resolve, and I make bold to assert that God helped me in emergencies. Mr. Wallace lingered around the house for some time, thinking I would come home. A watchful eye was kept on the path he must take on leaving the house. The moment for his departure came at last, and my heavy heart was lightened when I saw his retreating footsteps making their way homeward. I forsook my hiding-place and went home. To my great astonishment I learned that the scow with her load of wood was at the wharf, Mr. W. had sent one of his hands to assist in bringing it home. Shortly after I entered the yard I met Mr. Mansfield. His look and manner of speech indicated that something was wrong. He ordered me to go to the wharf immediately and "pitch the wood off the scow," he was afraid it would sink, "and get it home pretty quick!" Off I went, as usual, wondering what could be up now. My utmost endeavor was always to try and please him.

In the evening his son came to me, looking sad, and appeared anxious to say something. I was then working in the barn, and it was a convenient place for a kind of private interview, for no one at the house could see us. He informed me that his Uncle Wallace had that day urged his father to sell me to him, promising to give his boy, George, who was twenty-two years old, and $300 into the bargain. His father, after a little persuasion, had agreed to do so, though he did not want to part with me till after the second day of January next. At that time the papers were to be made out and signed. I gained further information from him concerning my future destiny-arranged by those ungenerous slave-holders. His uncle, H. Wallace, had a nephew living in New Orleans, a slave owner; he had a supply about once a year, and the time having arrived for a batch to be sent on I found I was to form one of the number, January being the month allotted for the transportation. By their unjust treatment they had forced me to form plans to make my escape from slavery. To New Orleans I did not intend to go if I could prevent it. These tidings caused me to devise means to put into execution an immediate flight. Whatever I was to do must be done at once. Christmas was drawing near, and New Year's was soon to follow; if alive, then my fate would be determined, and Wallace and Will had to decide that. Mr. Mansfield had put me out of his reach by making the bargain to sell.

CHAPTER III
ESCAPE FROM SLAVERY.

On the following Saturday night, after hearing this news, I hired a horse from an old colored man, Jim Willmer, for a bushel of oats. These were waste oats that I had saved from time to time from the horse's feed. That night I rode to George Town Cross Oats, the place of my nativity. I went in search of a colored man by the name of Joe Brown, arriving at his house about eleven o'clock that night. He had not gone to bed but was smoking his pipe; his wife had retired for the night, so everything was favorable as the business was highly important and only required two to discuss it at this time. I had known him ever since I was a boy, and he appeared kindly disposed toward me, so there was no feeling of scrupulousness in telling him what I intended and wanted. I related all my troubles to him, and finally told him that I wanted to get away and that he must assist me. He listened attentively to my statement and wishes, then he asked how many there were of us. I told him I thought I could bring two more with me. He arranged that I was to come to his house a week from that night, and if there were three to bring along with us nine dollars, and if we stood by him he would stand by us, landing us safely in Philadelphia. The coming Thursday from this night would be Christmas day, consequently the day of meeting would be in Christmas week during the holidays, when slaves are generally allowed to visit their friends for one or two days. Our business being over I left Joe Brown to enjoy his pipe a little longer and then retire to take his rest, while I joined the company of Jim Willmer's horse. There was not much time to linger on the road to meditate on the future. My faithful horse, moved by instinctiveness, made light of his burden and soon covered the distance between the two places. About two o'clock Sunday morning the horse was in the barn and I on my master's premises. Nobody knew that I had been from home, much less out of the city.

Mr. Mansfield had secured from his father's estate a young fellow by the name of Joshua. He had been with him about two years this Christmas. We were very intimate and I had placed the utmost confidence in him. Feeling he would not betray my secret, I ventured to inform him where I had been and what I had done. He felt much elated over the project and said he would go with me. We had a little money saved up that was earned by sawing wood and doing odd jobs at night for some of the neighbors, but that was not sufficient, therefore we had to enter into ways and means to secure the balance. We solicited work and were fortunate enough to find it, and by Saturday night our treasury showed the sum of $12. At last Christmas day had come-the bright and hopeful day of all Christendom when master and mistress with their friends were to make merry, and the poor slave to hope that he might be happy for a few hours at least. Mrs. Mary Mansfield attempted to make her slaves feel cheerful by giving them a Christmas breakfast, consisting of one quart of molasses, being one and one-third of a gill for each servant as there were six of us, about six pounds of sausage meat, which was the scrapings of the meat-block, and, after we had extracted the wood of the suffering block from it, we had, approximately, three pounds of meat, allowing each one-half of a pound. Along with this her bountiful heart permitted her to give a pan of middlings. This constituted our Christmas breakfast. While we were eating this festive meal Mr. Mansfield made his appearance and gave us each fifty cents, and at the same time told me I could go and see my father and mother on Saturday morning, but be sure and get back by Monday night without fail. If I had known that by casting decayed meat to the dog would have cost me so much trouble I would not have attempted it; and if he had known of my plans for making my escape he would not have given me money nor permission to visit the very place at the very time I wanted to go.

The young man George that I made mention of as coming to take my place, came to Chester-town on Friday, as he thought, to spend Christmas. I informed him that he was sold to Mansfield to take my place, and that the plot was to send me to New Orleans; that Joshua and myself had made arrangements to run away, and if he wanted to go with us he could do so. It did not take him long to decide to make one of the number. There was one difficulty in the way with him-he had no money. In order to obviate that difficulty Joshua and myself agreed to furnish it. I told George to return home and meet us at a certain place about nine o'clock with a boat to take us across the creek. Instead of my going away in the morning as permitted I remained until Saturday night, in order that we might be together, as Joshua was not acquainted with the route.

When night came we bade farewell to the Mansfield house with its cares and lashes, and started for the land of liberty and a city where we could breathe the refreshing air of freedom. When we reached our place of meeting, according to previous arrangement, about nine o'clock George was there with the boat waiting for us. The creek was soon crossed and our course was shaped for George Town Cross Oats, a distance of about twenty miles. We reached the town about two o'clock in the morning. The most interesting place to be found by us was the house of our guide, Joe Brown. To the horror of all we found Joe lying on the floor dead drunk. Joshua and George did not know Brown's failings; they became alarmed at the situation and talked strongly about going back home. This increased my anxiety considerably, for if they went back my plans would be destroyed and I returned into the hands of my enemies, or else hunted down and killed. I at last prevailed on them to go with me to my mother's and stay a few hours. This was Sunday morning, the distance was but half a mile, and we were soon sheltered and out of sight of Joe Brown. We stayed there all day concealed away up in the attic. This was a day of great suspense. No one could advise what would be the next best step to take. We were three helpless beings fleeing from the cruel chains of bondage.

To my happy surprise that afternoon Joe Brown put in his appearance. He did not remain long nor have much to say, but told us to meet him that night at Price's Woods at seven o'clock. As a signal of our meeting in safety he would give the sign by crying out, "yea! yo!" and we were to answer "Friend to the guard!" The place was well known to me and could be easily found. At seven o'clock, as near as we could judge, we were on the spot. The sign and countersign were exchanged, and we met. Brown was master of ceremonies. The first business to be done was the invocation and pledge. We all four knelt down and prayed and then took an oath that we would fight for each other till we died. This done, the next was to pay over the liberation money, nine dollars. Next came the hasty-eaten but substantial meal of bread and meat that was provided for us by our guide. We remained there half an hour. The ground was well covered with snow, making good sleighing.

The night of march had come, and with our anxious faces directed northward we started for Wilmington, Delaware, it being about thirty-five miles away. When we had arrived within eight miles of Wilmington, Brown took us to the house of an old colored man who was an acquaintance of his. I did not understand why he went there, but I judged it was to seek for information; and we did receive some very important news. The old man told him not to go any further on that road as there was a gang of body-snatchers waiting by the bridge to mob every colored person that came that way. He directed him to return about eight miles and take the first left hand road he came to, and that would bring him into Wilmington another way where he would not meet with any trouble. The old man's advice was heeded. We accordingly went back, and by the time we got there the grey dawn of morning began to appear. Day was breaking, and travelers like the three of this band had to seek a hiding-place while the glorious rays of the king of light prevailed, and men were abroad upon the face of the earth.

Fortune, thus far, had bountifully smiled on our path, and nature had lent us her aid, bidding us good-speed on our journey. As daylight lifted the sable curtain of night we saw but a short distance from us a dense wood, and we made for it in haste. On entering this forest we found a very large white oak tree that could not endure the mighty winds of the early fall, and it had been ruthlessly torn up by the roots before its leaves had fallen. There it lay, forming a complete arbor and place of safety. When the full light of day came, under it we crept, not knowing how long we were to remain, nor what might be the result. Joe Brown left us with strict orders to remain where we were until his return, that he was going to Wilmington. We had voluntarily placed ourselves under his care and direction for the safety of our escape, consequently it was no more than just that we should submit to his judgment and obey orders for the time being.

We stayed all day-or as long as daylight lasted. This was the greatest and most memorable day in this undertaking for liberty. Fugitives from slavery.

While lying on the cold ground under this tree, our "city of refuge," we were greatly surprised at seeing a number of fox hounds, numbering, I suppose, from twenty to fifty, running about the forest near to us. They were accompanied by about fifty men on horseback, who were all white. The reader may judge the terrible anxiety we had to endure. We were slaves fleeing from bondage, they were freemen, and to have fallen into their hands would have been so much added to their gain, and to us, perhaps, a more sorrowful condition than the one we were fleeing from. They rode and hunted after a fox throughout the whole day. Several times the fleeing fox made his unwelcome appearance under the tree that secreted us from the horsemen's view, and to my great astonishment I discovered we were lying over the hole that led to reynard's den. He made two or three attempts to get into the hole but we succeeded in beating him off, and the result was he did not return any more that day. Our anxiety became more and more intense as we recognized among the band of hunters some well-known faces, who, it cannot be claimed, were "a terror to all evil doers," but to all honest, trustworthy slaves. Had Mister Fox succeeded in entering the hole we would have been caught, and our jig would have been up sure. It was in this large, dense forest, in the State of Delaware, that I was led to see my own fate compared with that of the wild beast of the forest. True, there was some difference; the fox was free, and I was seeking for freedom; its pursuers were near by, but mine were, for all I knew, afar off. Our much-dreaded visitors remained in the neighborhood all day. It was almost dark before they relieved us of their presence. This was a day of "foes without and fears within," for while I wondered how this day's events would end from outward appearances, my two companions became so badly frightened that my words failed to comfort them. Their fears were so great that they determined to go back-not to the "flesh pots of Egypt," but to the stinted fare and cowhide of slavery. I determined differently. I longed for the home of the free. Finally, to quiet their fears, I promised if they would only keep silent I would take them back home.

After it got dark, I waited until the north star had risen, for I determined, as Joe Brown had not returned, that the journey should be continued. One day in a place like those woods, with two tired, discontented companions, was long enough to remain there. As my star of hope, the guide of the night, came fully in view, we started on our tramp, as the boys thought for our former home; but not so with me. I had gained some early knowledge of the north star for the express purpose for which I was now about to use it. An old man by the name of Charley Miller had told me where that star was, and if "I could follow it it would guide me north, that the Lord had placed it there to lead people out of slavery." I used it that night, believing what he told me was true. I followed it for about five miles, when, to my great astonishment, I met Joe Brown, our leader. He had with him another man who proved, afterwards, to be our guide for the remainder of the journey. Joe had with him something to appease our hunger and to cheer us on, in the substance of a boiled hog's head and a loaf of corn bread. He fed us, and we were truly glad to receive it, for we had been without food the whole day. The fear of being captured and returned to our masters, or else sold to new ones, had, no doubt, kept under the desire to eat. But now the evil threatenings of the day were over, and in the presence of help we could do justice to the nourishment our pilot had brought us. We stopped and talked for awhile, and Brown placed us under the care of this new comer, and he continued his journey homeward.

Having taken leave of our former friend and guide we continued to the goal of our ambition under the care of our new leader. There are a great many venturesome things a man will do, when determined to escape from danger or an evil, that he would not do when otherwise situated. To think that we had placed our fate in the hands of a man who was, to us, an utter stranger. The confidence that had been reposed in the integrity of Brown concerning our welfare was, simply, a transferable one. His deep interestedness in rescuing his race from the cruel chains of slavery, had established the faith that he would not permit us to be betrayed into the hands of a friend or advocate of the cruel institution. The experience of the past had taught us the lesson to trust and go forward, and forward we went. About midnight of that same day we passed by Wilmington unmolested by any one, and, as near as I can judge, it was three o'clock that morning when the dividing line that runs between the States of Delaware and Pennsylvania were crossed. No words can depict the joy and gratitude that filled the bosom of one who had, as it were-not rather as it actually was-stepped from bondage into liberty, from darkness into light.

I had no means of keeping the days of the month, but was fortunate enough to remember the day of the week. So it was on a Tuesday morning that our eyes rested on a State where liberty for the negro slave could be enjoyed. Perry Augustus, our guide, with much seeming satisfaction and delight, informed us that we had crossed out of slavery into freedom. We had had our faithful guides, and they had discharged their obligations to us to the letter; but I had not forgotten my early impressions of the existence of an ever kind Providence, for which gratitude should be shown, consequently I suggested that we should have a season of prayer and return thanks to God for this safe deliverance. The old man readily consented to the proposal, and we all knelt down on the snow-covered ground and offered up humble thanksgiving, and petitions for future protection and guidance, to the Great Supreme Ruler of heaven and earth. Those who have been under some heavy burden, weighing them down by continued torture and misery, when to their relief has come some happy event, or some sympathising friend who has removed the torturing evil, may form some idea of the felicity enjoyed by us on that memorable morning.

When the other two boys learned that we had been successful in crossing into the land of freedom, they became reconciled, and expressed themselves as being sorry for the unnecessary trouble they had caused me, especially while concealed in the forest. We journeyed on for a distance of about ten miles when we came to a place called New Garden. At this place we were made acquainted with an old man by the name of Nelson Wiggins. This we found also to be the resting place of Perry Augustus. Further developments showed that it was more than a resting place, it was a temporal home, a little heaven on earth for a fugitive. The old man had two daughters, who had charge of the house, as his wife was dead; one of these tender-hearted and benevolent ladies, with her father, bid us welcome and make ourselves at home. The invitation was readily accepted and we were comfortably housed and seated. Her agile step and busy hands were soon employed in preparing a breakfast for the weary travelers. When it had been prepared we were bid to partake of it. Breakfast over we were directed to go up stairs where we would find beds upon which to rest ourselves. The directions were soon followed, and we laid us down to rest and sleep, to dream of the past and plan for the future. We remained there all day.

The next night a great number of persons called to see us and congratulate us on our successful venture. Some of them we had known in by-gone days. This was delight added to pleasure. Companions in slavery once, now companions in freedom. Two days were spent in this state of ease and comfort, and on the third day it was deemed best that we should start out in search of employment. It being winter time, work, as a general thing, was very scarce; there did not seem to be anything to do in New Garden, so we concluded to make our way to Philadelphia.

CHAPTER IV
IN THE LAND OF FREEDOM.

On Saturday morning, we bid our kind host and benevolent daughters good-by and started on our journey. On account of not being acquainted with the road, we did not reach our destination until about seven o'clock that night. Going down (what we afterwards learned to be Market Street,) we found the markets open and crowded with people. I cannot say we were surprised, but I must confess that we were wonderfully frightened at seeing so many people at one place at the same time. The like was never seen by either of us before.

We continued down Market Street until we came to the ferry boat. Not daring to look to the right or left, we walked on board supposing all the while we were walking on the street. If it had not been for the guard chain at the bow of the boat, we would have walked overboard, when the waters below would have informed us of the blunder. Soon the whistle sounded, the engine was put in motion, and in a very short time we found ourselves in a little town called Camden. Here we wandered about for a short time, but at last concluded to seek the woods for shelter. We remained in seclusion all day Sunday, not daring to go to anybody's house for fear of being kidnapped or imprisoned. When night came, we started back by the same way we came, for we had neither money or friends. We knocked around there until the following Sunday; sometimes visiting somebody's house, and sometimes secreting ourselves in the woods.

One day we were successful in obtaining a job in cutting wood for a farmer who *very liberally* paid us for our services by giving us a supper and a night's lodging in his barn. Whether from the fear of us robbing his house, or for the welfare of our safe keeping I know not, but this I do know and well remember, that after we had gone into the barn, he locked the door and, I suppose, put the key in his pocket. By this ingenious precaution of safety, we had to remain whether we wanted to or not.

On the following Sunday during our travels, probably it would seem better to say wanderings, we met an old colored gentleman who very kindly took us to his home, a distance of about half a mile. Our feet at this time had become very much swollen and painful; and we were exceedingly tired. He proved to be "a friend in need as well as a friend indeed." He fed us sumptuously, and took special care of us. It was our happy lot to remain under his kind hospitality until the following Sunday morning. As was his custom, he went to church and should have us accompany him to the place of worship. After the service was ended, he announced in the church that he had with him three travelers, and wanted some of the brethren to care for them. A woman by the name of Mary Jackson arose and said that her employers wanted a man, and if one of them could go home with her, she thought she could get him a place. The opportunity was too good to be lost, and there was no time to be spent in thought. There was three of us, and one place presented, and it may well be imagined I hastened to speak up quickly, and said I would go. When she got ready we started, leaving my old companions in sorrow. We had to go a distance of five miles. The week's rest and good care, with the expectation of obtaining work afforded strength and cheer for the journey. This place proved to be Doe Run, in Chester County, and the man's name was James Pile, a farmer. When I saw him he told me he could give me work with a compensation of four dollars a month, board, lodging and washing. I accepted his terms, and made a bargain to work for him until the first of the coming April. One of the boys (my former associate) procured a situation similar to mine, and the other went to live with a colored family to cut wood for the winter. Just two weeks from the time we started from the land of slavery for that of freedom, we were settled down, independently working for our own bread, and choosing our own employers.

I remained in the employ of James Pile for nearly three months, and then renewed the agreement for an indefinite time, for eight dollars a month. I must mention something here with regard to a daughter of Mr. Pile's. It was a sight unseen by me in my southern home; and that was the daughter of a farmer or planter standing by the side of her father's workmen with a hay-fork in her hand, not idly standing by to see the work done properly, or that the men did not idle away their time, but to share in the labor of spreading and stacking the hay. When the time came to take it to the barn, she could do her part in pitching it on the cart. I continued to work on this farm until September.

When I left Mr. Pile's I went to a place called Chatham, where I hired myself to a man by the name of Sam Hooper, as a farmer; but my particular work was to thrash wheat. He agreed to pay me thirteen dollars a month with board and lodging. I did not remain in his employ very long. I worked around in different places until the month of April of the following year, sometimes thrashing wheat, sometimes quarrying stone and at other times cutting wood. On the 1st day of April, 1848, I entered into an agreement with Mr. David Chambers to work for him for eight months for ten dollars a month as a farmer. He made me his principal farm hand, and I continued in his service until the winter of 1849. On leaving this farm I went to live with a Mr. Joshua Pusey, another farmer, who agreed to give me fifty cents a day, a house to live in and two acres of planting land for my own use, six months firewood, with the use of a horse and team, and a horse to plough the ground. Perhaps some of my readers may wonder why these additions were made to my former contracts; why this house, this garden and firewood? I did not wonder at it, neither will you, dear reader, when I tell you I was making preparations to be married, and wanted a comfortable home for my bride and self. I anticipated great things. Once a slave, but now free and soon to be a married man. Yes, I was building airy castles in my imagination.

As the time advanced and I was to enter upon my new contract, my hopes grew brighter and my joys expanded. When my expectations were at their height, three slave-holders drove up from Maryland in a team and went to a neighboring house that was occupied by a colored man named Tom Mitchell, knocked the door in, took the man out and drove off with him, leaving his wife and children screaming for the loss of a fond, industrious husband and a loving father. This Tom Mitchell was like myself, a runaway slave and came from the same county as I did. That kind of work thoroughly frightened me, and I resolved that I would break the Pusey bargain and leave that region immediately.

Mitchell's captors were drovers, and knew him as a slave and of his whereabouts, and they made good use of their knowledge; they got fifty dollars for him. The Quakers, moved with sympathy for the wife and children, and knowing the worth of the captive, raised five hundred dollars and went south, purchased his freedom and brought him back.

I had agreed to be married March the first and go housekeeping April the first, but Mitchell's mishap upset my plans, at least for the time being.

I left and went to Philadelphia where I thought safety would be best secured. I worked there as a hod carrier up to September 12, then I went back to Chester county to fulfil my promise, not as to time, but to the person with whom I had agreed to marry. This was in 1849. After we were married, I took my wife to Philadelphia and went housekeeping.

I had not been long settled at housekeeping before the Fugitive Slave Law came into full force. One day while climbing the ladder with a hod of bricks on my shoulder, I looked down at the passers by, which was not an uncommon thing to do, and who should I see but the son of the man Wallace, who I had occasion to mention in my darkest days of slavery life. I continued my course upwards until I came to the staging. Discontent and fear would not permit me to remain there any time; to descend by the same way I ascended might prove dangerous, as young Wallace might still be somewhere near by, so I concluded to go down the back way. The first impression that came to me was to seek for counsel, so I at once notified some of the leading colored men, in whom I had confidence, of what I had seen and of my great dilemma. They immediately undertook to find out where he was stopping, and what his business was in this city, through lawyer Paul Brown. His business was soon found out and made known. He was searching for his runaway slaves, of whom I was one. As leader of the band, I was advised to make my way into Massachusetts, and that without much delay. "O the terror and curse of Slavery!" I concluded to sell out the little comforts that I had collected to make home pleasant, and leave for regions farther North, where the foot of the slave owner doth not tread. So I thought then, but came to know differently very soon afterwards. We sold what we could, and what we could not dispose of had to be given away.

Home was broken up, and travel or tramp was the order of the hour. I had a letter of recommendation given to me, which I was to present to a Mr. Gibbs, of New York City, on my arrival there, enroute for Boston, Mass. He was a worker in the Under Ground Railroad scheme, and was a colored man. We left Philadelphia by boat, and had a pleasant sail to New York. When we arrived, we did not meet Mr. Gibbs as we anticipated. He was late in getting to the boat. A hack driver came to me and said he worked for Mr. Gibbs. Being an entire stranger in that part of the country, and to the customs of the people, I was easily deluded. Depending on the truthfulness of the hackman, I handed my wife into the hack, put in my choice bundles, and then got in myself, leaving the driver to get the trunk and drive off. But while he was getting the trunk, Mr. Gibbs came and told us we were in the wrong hack, and to get out, to which the hackman objected. After considerable word wrangling, the driver and two other men jumped on Mr. Gibbs, and beat him unmercifully. During the contest I got out of the hack, removing my wife and bundles. The result was that the three hackmen were arrested and put in the lockup. Mr. Gibbs was beaten so badly that he had to be carried to his home. This was one of the unfortunate scenes that caused regret to fill my bosom, as it was on my account that a fellow-man, one of my own race, a helper to the poor tortured slave had been so cruelly handled. Another colored man took Mr. Gibbs' hack, and drove us to Bonaventure Street where we remained all night, to rest, to think and dream of the future, and to question what shall come next. We remained in this place until three o'clock the next day.

Mr. Gibbs was fortunate enough as to recover from the effects of the beating, so as to be out the next day. He came around to the place where we were stopping, and took us to the Fall River boat. He gave me a recommendation to a man in Boston by the name of Snowdon who would help me as he said. He informed me that it would cost four dollars each to go to Boston, Mass., and to give him the money and he would purchase the tickets. As a stranger I gave him the required sum supposing it was all right, as I was under his direction. He bought the tickets and gave them to me. We shook hands and bade each other good-by. The steam whistle blew, the moorings were loosed, the engine put in motion, the wheels rotated, and we were on our way to Boston. To my surprise I found, after we had reached the stream, that the tickets were second-class and not first, as Mr. Gibbs represented. He only paid two dollars each for them, and kept half the amount for himself. We had got beyond hailing power now; he was on the land and we on the water; perhaps he was out of the sight of the steamboat for all I knew. I pitied him when he got the beating, but on the discovery of deception, and his having taken unlawfully a part of my own hard earned and scanty means, the old Adam rose in my bosom, and destroyed the sympathy that was there, turning pity into passion and disdain. "Some men live by the sweat of their own brow, and some live by the sweat of others."

Not knowing the difference at first my wife and self went down in the first cabin and as we did not have the right kind of tickets, were ordered out. This was bad for my wife; I did not mind it so much. We had now been married about a month, and for her to be placed in that embarrassing state made me feel the condition more keenly. I paid one dollar more for her so that she could enjoy the comforts of a cabin passenger while I betook my weary self to the smoke-stack and there roasted my sides against the boiler in order to keep warm. So much for Mr. Gibbs' generosity. Onward glided our steamboat through the quiet sea, bearing us rapidly to a more northern home. Onward sped my wandering thoughts of a near future; what kind of a reception was awaiting me, and what would the prospects of employment and an income for labor be? The arrival of the boat at Fall River, the bustling crowd, the disembarking passengers aroused me from mental roamings. I had to join the busy throng and make my way to the cars, which was done and we were soon comfortably seated. The whistle blew and the train rolled out of the depot. My wife and I occupied seats together, thinking that all was right, but another trouble awaited me, another separation. Oh! those tickets. Oh! that man Gibbs. Our tickets were through ones, I did not understand the difference between first and second-class fares on the trains. I had learnt the method of boat traveling and was now about to take my first lesson on the railroad. The conductor was passing through the car collecting the tickets, everybody appeared to be all right until he came to me. I handed my ticket supposing I was like the rest, but soon found out there was a mistake. He told me to get up and go into the forward car, and wanted to know what I was "doing there." So I had to get up and leave; yes, to leave my wife to ride alone. When we arrived at Boston the first business my attention was directed to was to find Mr. Snowdon to whom I had a letter of introduction from Mr. Gibbs. After making some inquiry I was sadly disappointed to learn that he was dead. The gloom that began to spread over me was soon to disappear; the silvery lining was near by. A place of rest and shelter was providentially prepared for us in the hospitable residence of the late Lewis Hayden. We stayed with him two or three weeks, and being unsuccessful in obtaining work in that city we were sent to Worcester. In using the term *we* here is in reference to two young men, like myself seeking liberty and employment. I left my wife in Boston with the Hayden family. Mr. William C. Nell, a colored man, and an agent of the Anti-Slavery Society sent us to Worcester with letters of introduction to Mr. William Brown, now living and widely known. On arriving in this city, we soon found Mr. Brown and stayed with him that night. The next day we secured permanent lodging with Mr. Ebenezer Hemenway.

After jobbing around in various ways, I obtained steady employment on the farm of the late Major Newton on Pleasant Street. I worked on that farm until April 15, 1851, in company with Mr. C. B. Hadwin. Everything went on smoothly up to this time, when those tormenting slave-holders, who had come that winter, began to make themselves very conspicuous in hunting for slave property. The poor despised negro slave was a valuable article. Dollars and cents with thousands of miles of hard travel and privations were no objects of consideration in the long chase and capture of a runaway slave. This hunting slave fever got so high that our sympathizing friends advised me to leave at once and go to Canada. The two men that came with me from Boston, met and consulted at Abram Howland's store what had best be done. To remain here, there would be a chance of capture, to leave, there would be an opportunity to escape. The latter we agreed on, making our departure a speedy issue. However, before going I hired rooms and had my wife come here to live; for I thought her opportunities to get along would be better than in Boston.

On the fifteenth day of April, 1851, the three of us took the train to Montreal, Dominion of Canada. We left on Saturday and arrived at our destination about eleven o'clock Sunday. The river being frozen over we had to cross on the ice on runners, but I did not know of the change until I got to the depot. The snow was packed up so high in the streets that pedestrians could not see each other from opposite sidewalks. It was soon discovered that Montreal was not the place to welcome the laboring man when a stranger; for there was nothing doing there, or anything we could find to do that would give us an honest living. Consequently we did not stay there but a few days. We went from there to a place called Kingston, on the Lake, and stayed there but one day as the prospects of work was far worse than in Montreal.

Next we went to Toronto where we found the climate warmer, and general business a little better. We concluded to find a boarding place and try our luck there. The place we sought was soon obtained, and agreed to pay three dollars a week for board and lodging. Near the end of the second week after being there, we procured work with an old colored man who done a trucking business. At this time he had taken a contract to move a building, and being in want of assistance, he hired the three of us at rates of fifty cents a day. Just enough to meet our boarding charges. The distance the house was to be moved was about two miles. Work was begun by employers and employees arduously, and progressed as we thought safely. Well it did for nine days, but on the tenth day, a sad disaster was in store for us, and another draw-back to poor Isaac's progress. On this day we came to the descent of a hill over which our road lay. The old rope was not new nor none of the best, so when the weight of the building becoming greater and greater by the declivity of the road, the hempen or flaxen cords were strained beyond their strength. At last they snapped, they break asunder; and away went the house without the aid of man or beast down the hill. With almost breathless astonishment, we stood gazing at the sliding object, when suddenly a collision is observed, a crushing noise is heard, the house has collapsed and gone to pieces.

The man who owned the building sued the contractor for damages, got judgment against him; and, also, got all the old man owned, horses and trucks. So we unfortunates got nothing for our work and were in debt for board to the amount of six dollars, and nothing to pay it with. It was a sad loss to us. Our clothes and all we had were held in payment for indebtedness. They were placed under lock and key. Among my clothing was my wedding suit that cost me fifty dollars, also a valuable pair of boots. We quitted boarding at that place at once and went to Queen's Bush, about seven miles from Toronto. There we made arrangements with a man to cut fire wood, at fifty cents a cord-four feet long. He kept a store and promised to furnish us with meat, bread and potatoes; our working tools such as axes, mauls, wedges, &c., &c., were to be had from him. After all necessary arrangements had been perfected, we went into the woods, cut down some logs and put up a log house, covering it with bushes, old boards and slabs which made it pretty tight. With our rude home and home comforts provided, we went into chopping firewood in good earnest. When we had chopped about one hundred cords, we proposed to make a settlement, and get our money and visit Toronto to redeem our clothes. The employer's account against us was fifteen dollars, which left a balance due us of about thirty-five dollars, which would be more than enough to carry out our honest plan. But instead of receiving that amount we only got fifty cents a piece; yes that was all we got. This was on Saturday and we intended to spend Sunday in Toronto. Being thus disappointed, we concluded to spend the Sabbath in the lonely woods, as we could not then better our condition. He promised to pay us in full the next following Saturday. Monday morning we resumed our work, looking forward to be amply rewarded for the disappointment by the end of the next six days' labor. On went the days and up and down went our toiling hands cutting, splitting and stacking. At last Saturday arrives, and we appear before our employer for settlement. It is said, "The last state of that man was worse than the first." This saying was fully verified in this man, for his last state was worse than the first one, and this Saturday was worse than the last one, for we did not get one cent. We found out that he did not own the land on which we worked, but that he himself was hired by a man in Toronto to cut and deliver this wood at the steamboat pier. This Saturday I determined to go to Toronto myself. I left the other boys in the woods and started for the city of Toronto. I began to make search for the man that had the wood cut or owned the land on which we worked, and found he was a steamboat owner. I learned from him that the man who was doing the work for him had been all paid up, and there was not anything due him. Even the horses and carts that were used in drawing the wood were all owned by the same man-that is the owner of the steamboat. He told me if my companions and myself would go back to work chopping wood, he himself would see us paid, but we would have to be the losers of what he had already paid the agent. While we were studying to be honest in paying our board bill; another was studying to dishonestly rob us of strength and labor.

While in Toronto this time, I sought out a friend with whom I had become acquainted with when there before, and got him to write a letter for me to Mr. Joshua Spooner, who was then living on the Major Newton farm in Worcester, Mass., and asking him to send me six dollars as I wanted to come home to Worcester. Within five days from the time I sent the letter his reply came containing the amount I sent for. I did not go back to the woods again. Disgust and discouragement prevented me from laboring for a man who cheated me out of my just due. I left the other boys there, how long they remained I do not know. During these five days of interval between the sending and receiving the Worcester letter, I did a job for the man who had my clothes in bond or locked up, which amounted to three dollars. I left in his hands two, on account, and kept one for myself.

I went to the steamboat pier every day at four o'clock, and became familiar with the faces of the different boats that plied between Toronto and Rochester, N. Y. On the receipt of the money from Worcester, I immediately paid the balance of four dollars due on board bill, redeeming my clothes, and leaving me two dollars for traveling expenses. As soon as I got my goods out of the possession of my former boarding master, I bade him good-by and started for the pier. This was on the night of the same Friday I received the money.

I sought the captain of the boat that left Saturday evening, and asked him to allow me to work my way to Rochester, N. Y. He quickly replied: "No; he would not allow it." I took out the letter I had received that day from Worcester, Mass., containing an account of my wife's sickness, and requesting him to read it. He did so, and I informed him how I was compelled to pay away what money I had received. The letter with my pleadings moved his sympathy towards me; he turned and said, I could go but that I should have to work every hour of the time. I said his sympathy was towards me, but that only went as far as being on board the steamboat; I had to pay by hard work and no sleep. I was content to comply with his demands; I had started for home, and could not pay for my traveling expenses with money, so would have to pay it by labor. He told me to go to the steward and get my supper, which I did. That was Friday night, and Saturday morning I went to work helping to load the steamboat. This work continued until four o'clock in the afternoon, the appointed time for the boat to start.

At the hour designated we left the pier and was stopping at different places off and on all night, putting off and taking on freight and passengers until eight o'clock Sunday morning, when we arrived in Rochester. I had not taken off my clothes or taken a wink of sleep all night. Being tired and sleepy after a day and night's hard toil, I took a conveyance and went to hunt for a lodging house, and my search was soon found. I went to bed and slept soundly until four o'clock in the afternoon. When I landed in Rochester I was the owner of two dollars and no more. This was the extent of my cash account. It cost me twenty-five cents for conveyance, and fifty cents for lodging and dinner. Here I was in the western part of New York state, miles from the city of Worcester, Mass., my place of destination, with one dollar and twenty-five cents to purchase a railroad ticket.

I went to the depot and inquired the fare to Worcester, and was informed it would be fifteen dollars. My readers who may have been placed in such a predicament can have some idea of the situation and can extend some sympathy; and those who have not may draw upon their imagination and perhaps gain a faint knowledge of the condition of an almost penniless traveler. With wishful eyes I gazed at the departing trains with their freight of living beings, but that was only vexation of spirit to me, and a force of circumstances beyond my control.

Worcester and my sick wife loomed up before me demanding my appearance. To purchase a ticket was impossible, to beg one was decidedly out of the question. At last I concluded it was no use of tarrying any longer in that place. My feet and legs had done me good service in my flight from Chestertown, Maryland to Philadelphia, Penn. I now made up my mind to trust to them at this time to reach my home, so off I started with the determination to walk to Worcester. It was about half past five P. M. with my knapsack on my back, I started on my long tedious march without friend, guide or compass. I followed the railroad track going east as a conductor on the way. Soon night began to spread its dark mantle around me, yet undismayed, I pressed forward deeply occupied with thoughts of the future. Midnight came in its stillness finding me still widening the distance between myself and the Rochester depot. Midnight passes, the small hours of the morn increase, until at last the light of a new day begins to dawn upon the world, when men begin to rise from their warm comfortable beds after a night of refreshing sleep. In rapid flight of early dawn, the king of day, the centre of celestial light, rises in majestic splendor over the eastern hills, indicating the cardinal point to which my journey lay. With it came the cheer that one night had passed away, shortening the distance between the starting point and that of my destination. At eight o'clock to my surprise, I found I had covered a distance of seventy-five miles that night. A night's walk without a halt to rest or refresh. As the day began to grow I determined to change my road of travel. I now abandoned the railroad for the tow-path, thinking to facilitate the travel; but I soon found out I did not get along so fast. My feet became sore and lame, the continual walking was beginning to manifest itself on my physical constitution; but ambition with the force of will obviated the pain and urged the man of suffering and disappointment onward.

After continuing in this condition for two or three days, the captain of a canal boat asked me how I would like to ride one of the horses at night, and remain on the boat during the day. The proposal had its charms for me. There would be a chance for sleep during the day, there was an opportunity for a good warm meal, and at night to sit on the horse's back. The offer was accepted and I went on board the boat.

The first night passed off without anything to cause alarm or to hinder the work. In the morning I did a little work on the boat, got my own breakfast and sought to lie down and sleep. On the second night I resumed my task, mounted the horse, who with slow, steady tread, tramped out the time allotted him. Night wore on, all on board the boat was stillness; all had retired for the night to enjoy Nature's refreshing invigorator, sleep. As the light of early dawn lifted the curtain of night, so that surrounding objects could be distinctly descerned, it brought another gleam of light, for I was so much farther advanced on my journey, and had enjoyed a little sleep and rest. We had reached Utica, N. Y. The time would soon come when I should dismount my horse to betake myself to the boat for rest and sleep. Sometimes it is remarkable easy to plan out a few hours or days, but they are not as soon brought to perfection. Difficulties in some form are apt to appear before us and impede our progress. Surprises are constantly-well nearly so-approaching us. There is the agreeable and disagreeable. Well there was a surprise in reserve for this morning. I leave my reader to judge whether it was a disagreeable or agreeable one after I have related it.

As we drew near a bridge under which we had to pass, I cast my eyes upwards and to my utter surprise and astonishment what should I see but the form of a man looking down on me. How quickly I remembered those well known features. The man who five years ago was my master, who held me in the bonds of slavery, who had cut and slashed my back; from whom I had fled to enjoy the pure air of liberty.

He did not recognize me, but I did him, and that was enough for the hunted. I at once took in the whole situation of the present and future. I felt positive he was hunting for me. To remain long exposed to his gaze would cause me danger and trouble. I dropped my head to conceal my face from his longing, anxious eyes, and as soon as I had gone out of his sight, I dismounted the horse, went on board the boat, got my little bundle of goods and left the boat and horses in a great hurry. I did not see the captain or any of the hands as they were all asleep, and I had no time to call them. The horses were left to take care of themselves, and go on of their own accord, as far as I know. These moments with me were most precious for self preservation. The hunter was on my track, had seen but not scented out my course. The necessity of the hour compelled me to be as agile as a hare and as cunning as a fox.

I took to the main road intending to continue my journey on foot the remainder of the way. Once more I found myself alone, with the end of my destination before me and not the means to buy the cheapest means of travel; depending upon the charity of the world. With a spirit of determination and courage I pressed forward hour after hour in the cheering light of day. Night overtakes me, a weary traveler, without shelter or food. To lie down and rest I could not, in fact rest had no charms for me in this lonely journey. Worcester and those who were all to me in this life were anxious companions of my nocturnal travel. Saturday night I found myself at the railroad station in the city of Albany, N. Y. Crossing the ferry, a thunder storm coming up suddenly, I took shelter in an inviting freight car, which was standing conveniently near the landing. I sat down, or rather lay down, to rest and await the conclusion of the storm, but tired and weary nature asserted her rights, and I was soon fast asleep. When I awoke I found the car had been traveling, and I became somewhat alarmed, as I did not know the route I had been going, or where I might possibly be. But my doubts were soon dispelled, for the car stopped at a way station and switched, so getting out, and looking up to the sun I soon discovered that I had been traveling in the right direction, and upon inquiry found that I had come ten miles due east on my direct road to Worcester. The day being Sunday I strayed out to a camp meeting of colored people and had a pleasant time with them.

Finding my efforts had been so satisfactory, my hopes revived, and my courage enlivened at the thought of soon ending this toilsome labor. Starting off again Sunday night, I continued my travel until reaching Worcester, Mass., which was on the second day of July, 1851, just two weeks from the day I went on board the steamboat at Toronto, Canada. The relief of over exertion, of physical fatigue, mental anxiety and the privation of natural comforts are better felt and appreciated in thought than expressed in words.

Having again joined my family and friends, I concluded to remain in Worcester, Mass., or I may say to make it my home, as I had not found a place in preference. It was not long before I found plenty of good employment and benevolent sympathizers, and for forty-three years Worcester has been my residence.

CHAPTER V
A FLYING VISIT TO HAYTI.

Being at this age a man of an enterprising turn of mind and inclined to be somewhat of an adventurer, or, as some of my readers will say, only extending an acquired habit, I was ready to enter upon any new enterprise that might hold out inducements for benefiting my condition or the advancement of the human family. For the purpose of furthering those ambitious ideas I sought the fraternity of the best and most popular societies as a means to carry out that end.

Coming thus far in my history there is a portion of my life that is connected with a foreign land, and I can not refrain from adding it here. In the year 1859, Mr. James Redpath went to Hayti, and while there made arrangements to emigrate as many colored people from the United States to that island as he could induce. He returned to this country and through his influence a large number of persons became interested in the emigration scheme, that during that year he sent two or three vessel loads of human freight to the foreign isle. Early in the following year he sent more from New York, Providence and Boston. He succeeded in making arrangements so that all emigrants should be landed free of charge. He also further arranged with the Haytian government that such emigrants arriving in their country should receive sixteen days' provisions from the time of landing. I heard so much about this country and the prospects it held out to such enterprisers, and the possibility of soon becoming well-to-do there that I concluded there might be a possible chance for me to enjoy a part of its wealthy production. Time and heresay increased the desire, and I finally thought of going to see the land of milk and honey for myself. I wrote to Mr. Redpath, the agent, informing him of my intentions, and also stating that I preferred to pay my own expenses. His answer came stating that my application and wishes were accepted. No time was wasted in making the necessary preparations for the voyage. May 14th, 1860, found me with an anxious number standing on Liverpool wharf, Boston, Mass., waiting to embark on the schooner Pearl, commanded by captain Porter. Our vessel was not of sufficient capacity to accommodate the number about to go. There were seventy-five emigrants, five cabin passengers, including myself, and a crew consisting of five; too large a number to be assigned to a small schooner. About 5 P. M., we sailed out of the harbor in search of southern islands and southern wealth.

That night we experienced a very severe gale, lasting the whole night. The next morning, Sunday, found us in much sadness. It revealed the horrors of the previous night. Not in the rented sails or strained ropes, but its deadly effects upon a human creature. Among the number that embarked with us the day previous was a young lady full of bright anticipations and apparently hale and hearty, going to seek a living in a foreign land, now lying before us cold and lifeless. The howling winds, the raging billows and the rolling vessel during the night proved a monster too strong for her. Overpowered with exhaustion and fright of being a castaway upon the ocean deep, she falls a victim to death. Others became severely ill and were made speechless for a time from the ordeal of that night. I considered myself to be one of the fortunate ones in not experiencing any sickness or fear. During the gale our two small boats and galley were washed away from the deck. Sunday was a beautiful day, all that could be desired to raise our hopes and quell our fears of the return or approach of another such storm. During the voyage of four weeks and four days after the Saturday night's storm nothing eventful occurred; all was pleasant and cheerful. As is always customary for travelers seeking for homes in distant lands, speculation and expectation were the chief subjects of conversation.

When the land of our destination was reached, and owing to the lateness of the day, the captain was prevented from having the vessel securely moored to the pier that night, consequently our anchorage had to be about half a mile from the shore. As we were not in a sheltering harbor, we became exposed to the gales. As the angry elements united to bid us farewell from Massachusetts shores, so apparently they had agreed to welcome us to Haytian lands; for that night the winds became exceedingly angry, tossing and forcing our craft before it with such pressure that our fears and anxieties of safety were greatly increased. At last the increasing power of the gale caused the chain to part; but fortunately the wind blew from the shore and we were driven to sea. If the wind had been blowing from a different direction, it is probable that the schooner and all on board would have been lost that night. It took us two days to return and cast a second anchor and prepare for landing.

When we went ashore the natives received us very hospitably, which made us feel that we were not intruders, but welcome aliens. The weather was so exceedingly hot that it seemed impossible for living creatures to exist there. Of course we just arrived from a northern climate, and would consequently feel the change more readily than one who had become accustomed to it. On inquiry I learned that the death rate averaged from three to four per day. This was not very pleasing information to be made known to those who came seeking a permanent home. At a place called St. Marks there were settled about five hundred persons that had emigrated to Hayti at different times. The natives were mostly of Roman Catholic persuasion. Sunday with them was a great day. I suppose it might have been termed a weekly holiday; and they seemed to have an order of exercises for the day, and it was somewhat after the following order: first they would turn out by thousands, have a military drill; second, they would all go to church and perform their religious services; third, then would follow a dance. The rest of the day was then spent in all kinds of amusements. These exercises seemed significant to their habits and customs. The drill indicative to their war-like habits, the church the respect, if not the piety for the Deity; the dance as tokens of victory achieved, ending the day with diversion to fill out the time.

The women do or are made to do the work of men at home and general laboring. They also had to do a part of military duty, such as keeping guard in defence of the country in times of peace as well as in war. The people are very small or generally of medium size, and of a general healthy appearance. I did not see any cripples among them. The women are not forced to do hard work because they are bad looking; for on the contrary they are handsome. Among the peculiarities of the people may be noticed the manner in which they slay animals for food. When an ox is to be prepared he is taken to the burying ground, and there it is beaten until all the blood is out of it. If it is a chicken they first pray over it. If it is a hog, its head is chopped off on a log of wood. These seemed to be the general methods of slaughtering.

The fertility of the island was of the highest order. It was so productive that cotton and all kinds of vegetables grew without any great degree of labor to cultivate. To encourage emigration, and to introduce foreign enterprises and customs into Hayti, the government had given to all emigrants the exclusive use of Artibinique River, and the lands surrounding it. This settlement was about five miles from St. Marks. Each emigrant was entitled to sixteen acres free. One day four others with myself hired horses, and rode out to see the situation and examine the land. As to the land everything seemed hopeful, but when we came to talk with some that had settled there, it was found that something more than good soil was needful to ensure safety and to produce grain. We were told that the winds at times were so terrific that houses were carried away before them, and it was almost impossible to keep oneself on the land during the gale.

After long and patient struggling of those hard determined toilers of the soil, the whole project proved a failure and had to be abandoned. Not only were the winds a barrier to their prospects, but the burning rays of the sun, was more than strangers could live under. At times (and that frequently) the thermometer would register 175° in the shade. During my stay there I was taken very ill, and at one time life was despaired of by those who went out with me. Some of those kind-hearted fellow travelers stood around my sick bed expecting every moment to see me breathe my last. While I was lying in this uncertain condition, one of the native women passing by my door took in the situation; for I was partially unconscious and my lips firmly closed, so I learned afterwards. She took the peel of an orange, (the white inner part) and poured boiling water on it, opened my mouth and poured it in. In less than ten minutes my lips began to move, and from that time a change for the better was manifested, and my restoration to health soon followed. I have great reason in commending the skill of that woman who saved my life, and my body from being buried beneath the burning sands of a tropical clime. I believed then and have since, in that illness my end was near, but restoration was possible, and it came by the hand of a Haytian doctress.

When recovering from this fit of sickness, one Sunday morning I took a walk out, slowly measuring my feeble steps, while my eyes roved from one object to another, and they were attracted to the various flags floating in the air, representing all, or nearly all the nations. The sight of them enlivened me and as I paused to view them closely there seemed to be one that surpassed them all for splendor; and that was the stars and stripes of America. Its grandeur was such that I felt a spirit of national pride for it, that I had never felt before.

After recovering from my sickness, I turned my thoughts more towards this emigration scheme determined to find out if it was good or evil, if there was anything in it or not for the good of my race. There was a large number that had been misled to emigrate there; they had no money to carry them there, and no means of procuring any to bring them back. If they had been required to pay their way out there, they could not have gone. After getting there they could not work or live, because they were not acclimated, and many died. With the knowledge of all this before me, what must be my conclusion? That it was misleading of the innocent by the false representation of a cunning plotter. To me it was false and evil to the race, and by me it was denounced. My conclusions were made and they were, if possible, to return home to Worcester, Mass., and so I informed my companions and others. As Captain Porter had not sailed for the north, but would do so on the latter part of July, I determined to be one of the number that his craft should convey home. Before leaving I had placed in my hands three hundred and twenty-five letters from the emigrants to be forwarded to their friends in different parts of America. They all went through the Post Office in Worcester to their destination. Their personal contents were not known to me, but my return and the expressions contained in these letters broke up Haytian emigration. When Mr. Redpath found out my determination to return, he persuaded and threatened against my leaving; and when he found his arguments were of no avail, he tried to buy me over to his cause, but it was all in vain, for I was determined that this scheme should be exposed and destroyed. To carry out this intention I published it in the Worcester daily papers showing that it was only a premature graveyard for the race. That out of the five thousand who emigrated there under the Redpath scheme, two-thirds fell victims to disease and death.

The superstitious would have said that the waiting and welcome gales were bad omens. Well they seemed so for the fury of the elements set their fury against it. The homeward voyage was not like the outward for we returned on the last day of August to the city of Boston, Mass., on peaceful seas and gentle winds, which characterized the whole passage.

When I arrived at my home, I returned thanks to the Lord for his mercy to me, sparing my life through the perils of the storm, from the perils of the heat, through the perils of sickness, and from the perils of death. I then made up my mind that Worcester should be my future home, and here I should dwell until the end of my days.

Made in the USA
Monee, IL
08 July 2026